LANGUAGE BEHIND BARS

PAUL CELAN'S *SPRACHGITTER*

Translated by David Young

MARICK PRESS

LIBRARY OF CONGRESS CATALOGUING IN PUBLICATION DATA

Marick Press
Language Behind Bars
Paul Celan's Sprachgitter
Translated by David Young
Poetry Collection in English
ISBN: 978-1-934851-48-7

Copyright © by Marick Press 2012
Design and typesetting by Alison Carr
Cover design by Marick Press
Cover art by Gisèle Celan-Le Strange
Printed and bound in the United States

Marick Press
P.O. Box 36253
Grosse Pointe Farms
Michigan 48236
www.marickpress.com

Distributed by
Small Press Distribution
and
Ingram

Marick Press is an independent literary press that publishes fine literature.
Marick Press is a registered 501 (c) 3 non-profit organization and we
rely on public and private funding to carry out the mission of publishing
annually 6-8 titles in both hardcover and paperback covering a broad
spectrum of topic that range from literary non-fiction, creative non-fiction,
poetry, fiction and reprint of previously published titles.

Marick Press is not-for-profit literary publisher, founded to preserve the best
work by poets around the world, including many under published women poets.

Marick Press seeks out and publishes the best new work from an
eclectic range of aesthetics —work that is technically accomplished,
distinctive in style, and thematically fresh.

CONTENTS

Introduction ... *v*

I
Stimmen/Voices ... 2/3

II
Zuversicht/Trust ... 12/13
Mit Brief und Uhr/With Letter and Clock ... 14/15
Unter ein Bild/Under a Picture ... 16/17
Heimkehr/Homecoming ... 18/19
Unten/Below ... 20/21
Heute und Morgen/Today and Tomorrow ... 22/23
Schliere/Streak ... 24/25

III
Tenebrae/Tenebrae ... 28/29
Blume/Flower ... 30/31
Weiss und Licht/White and Light ... 32/33
Sprachgitter/Language Behind Bars ... 36/37
Schneebett/Snow-Bed ... 38/39
Windgerecht/According to the Wind ... 40/41
Nacht/Night ... 42/43
Matière de Bretagne/Matière de Bretagne ... 44/45
Schuttkahn/Rubbish Barge ... 48/49

IV

Köln, am Hof/Cologne, at the Hof ... 52/53

In die Ferne/Into the Distance ... 54/55

Ein Tag und noch Einer/One Day and Then Another ... 56/57

In Mundhöhe/At Mouth Level ... 58/59

Eine Hand/A Hand ... 60/61

Aber/But ... 62/62

Allerseelen/All Souls ... 64/65

Entwurf einer Landschaft/Sketch for a Landscape ... 66/67

V

Ein Auge, Offen/En Eye, Open ... 70/71

OBEN, GERÄUSCHLOS, die/

    OVERHEAD, NOISELESS, those ... 72/73

DIE WELT, zu uns/THE WORLD, joining us ... 76/77

EIN HOLZSTERN, blau/A WOODSTAR, blue ... 78/79

Sommerbericht/Summer Report ... 80/81

NIEDRIGWASSER, Wir sahen/

    LOW-LYING WATER. We saw ... 82/83

Bahndämme, Wegränder, Ödplätze, Schutt/Railway

    Embankments, Roadsides, Vacant Lots, Rubbish ... 84/85

Engführung/Stretto ... 88/89

INTRODUCTION
David Young

From its title on, Paul Celan's 1959 volume *Sprachgitter* centers on problems of communication, a crisis of language that involves both the poet and his readers. We can call this crisis historical, stemming from the events of World War Two and the Holocaust (or "Shoah," a preferred term). Celan had lost both his parents to the Nazi death machine and he was determined to try to restore integrity to the language that the Third Reich had corrupted and appropriated.

We can also call the crisis existential, suggesting that the difficulties of communication, while specific to World War Two, are finally endemic to language and the human condition. We can even call it metaphysical, since Celan uses it to question matters of belief in God, especially with respect to orthodox Judaism.

Whatever their sources and contexts, these same problems accompany, of course, any attempts at translation. And any translator of Celan must address them. The language crisis is something of a two-edged sword. It may often feel as though the difficulties of translation have been compounded, but it can also feel as though the original poems, and their author, are prepared to extend sympathy, and a sense of common ground, to anyone trying to translate them.

The book's title, for example, resists any single English version. "Sprach" means both "language" and "speech," and I have chosen the first of these mainly because it is the more comprehensive of the two. But that choice has meant losing the strong implication of speakers and speaking, always crucial to this poet's sense of the action and character of his poems. Still, *language* is the larger and more constant arena of crisis and it is in that fraught space that Celan courageously stakes his claim to be a poet.

As for "-gitter," Celan has characteristically coined a new word by combining it with "Sprach." A *Gitter* is a grille, or lattice, or grating, or grid. While it can, for instance, suggest the barrier between the priest and the communicant in the confessional, or the grating through which nuns were allowed communication with the world outside the convent, its main implication for Celan seems to be that of imprisonment. In the poem that gives the book its title, language and speech are bound or confined, like a prisoner's eye peeking out from behind a grille or grid or bars. Since imprisonment in English and American parlance is mainly a matter of being behind bars rather than behind a grill or grid, I have chosen that option, and its implications, in my translation of the title. *Language Behind Bars* captures part of what *Sprachgitter* suggests, though not all of it. *Language-Bars*, or *Behind Language Bars*, might be appropriate as well, if those phrases didn't suggest bars made out of language. Other possibilities, some of which previous translators and commentators have used, include *Speech-Grille* and *Speech-Grid*.

Celan may have had in mind Rilke's famous panther poem, where the caged beast paces obsessively and seldom sees beyond the cage-bars that confine it. When it does, a moment of electrifying recognition occurs, affecting the watcher as well as the animal; Celan may be expressing the hope that, at least occasionally, his poetic language can pass through the bars of its crisis and imprisonment – a compound of historical destruction, anti-Semitism, and his sense of being an outsider – and reach his reader/listener.

Rilke makes another appearance, at least to this listener's ear, in the opening sequence of the volume, where the word *Stimmen* [*Voices*], tolls like a bell to open each section, recalling this passage from the First Duino Elegy:

> Stimmen. Stimmen. Höre, mein Herz, wie sonst nur
> Heilige hörten: daß sie der riesige Ruf
> Aufhob von Boden . . .

(Voices, voices.

Listen, my heart

as only the saints

have listened

for a gigantic call

to lift them

right off the ground . . .)[1]

Rilke contrasts himself with those saints. He can't expect to hear, or bear, God's voice, so he must instead attend to the soft report "that grows out of silence," coming from "those who died young."

If Rilke finds himself rewriting the possibilities of Christian visionary experience, Celan takes the contrast further still. The voices that cut and disrupt and thread themselves through his world come mostly from all the dead of the Shoah and the war. They are more ambiguous and even hurtful, mixing past and present, living and dead, sorrow and joy, loss and renewal, and they make his task as a poet endlessly difficult. If the voices can "make your heart / turn back into your mother's heart" then they represent, as the poem goes on to assert, a wound that will not scar over or heal. The voices are everywhere and nowhere, and the poet can neither control them, tune them out, nor let them dominate. He must learn how to live with them, in a continuous, painful, but thrilling sense of their choric presence.

* * *

From this difficult recognition, the volume moves forward into an often fragmentary and rebarbative world, where poetry and even beauty are possible only when they do not refuse the melancholy

---

1 My translation, W.W. Norton, 1978, 1992, 2006, p. 35.

recognition of all the dead, of all that has been lost to the world. Sometimes the poems rise toward a cautious visionary ecstasy; sometimes they resemble tentative prayers. Always they show us that, for both the poet and the reader, anything "poetic" will be hard-won, temporary, and ambiguous. The poet will do his best to find meaning and value in his haunted, difficult world, but we cannot expect him to gloss over or falsify the truth of his history and existence. That is why we find him a difficult companion, but it is also why we come to value his company as we do almost nobody else's from his time and place.

Sometimes we find him in a familiar setting, such as an art exhibit, encountering a kindred spirit, as when he gazes at Van Gogh's last painting:

UNDER A PICTURE

Ravenswarmed wheatsea.
Which heaven's blue? The one below? Above?
Arrow that came later, shot from the soul.
Louder whirring. Nearer glowing. Both worlds.

This seems to recognize that Van Gogh saw the world both in terms of its physical reality and its visionary presences, and that his paintings managed to capture that double sensibility. For Celan, struggling with a similar duality of perception, the encounter with the painter, even when the latter was at the verge of suicide, brings a kind of comfort. In fact, as I have suggested elsewhere, Celan seems to be contradicting the popular reading of the painting as full of despair and suicidal thoughts. It is not that Van Gogh is forecasting his own death; it is that his perception is so ecstatic, so full and complete, that he gives us access to states we would not otherwise be able to enter and tolerate.[2]

Even something as natural and inevitable as a snowfall can become, for this poet, as the poem immediately following suggests, a "Homecoming":

> Snowfall, thicker and thicker,
> dove-colored, like yesterday,
> snowfall, as if you were still asleep now.

The "you" addressed here must be multiple; it includes the dead, so peaceful that they seem to be sleeping and might wake up, and the speaking self, experiencing a dreamlike reality:

> Widely layered white.
> On top of it, endlessly,
> the sleigh-tracks of the lost.

The dead are present through their absence; only their tracks are visible, but for the speaker they are straining, also, to be perceived:

> Underneath, sheltered,
> straining upward,
> that which hurts the eyes,
> hill after hill,
> invisible.
>
> On each,
> brought home to its present,

2 "'To Be Written Under a Picture': The Poet as Allegorist and Visionary." FIELD: Contemporary Poetry and Poetics. Number 71, Fall, 2004. pp. 19-24.

an "I" that has slipped away into muteness:
wooden, a post.

The very fenceposts mutely testify to this witness that their subjects
("I" after "I" after "I"), refuse to be buried and forgotten. In his snowy
landscape, they make themselves known and felt. The poem closes
with an ambiguous image of the white flag of surrender. Who is sur-
rendering? The poet, or the dead whom he can still perceive?

There: a feeling,
carried here on the icy wind,
fastening its dove-, its snow-,
colored cloth flag.

This little poem, composed around Christmas, 1955, bears an inter-
esting relation to Frost's "Stopping by Woods on a Snowy Evening,"
which Celan had translated into German. There's a well-known mo-
ment in his version, when the English word "downy" is rendered as
"erdwärts," literally "earthward." Scholars argue about whether the
mistake was inadvertent or deliberate. Given Celan's constant sense
of the earth's meaning, its chthonic presences, a darkening gesture
would seem to be a fairly deliberate possibility.[3] Just as with Van
Gogh, Celan is seeking a kindred spirit who can share some of his
sense of the ubiquitous presence of death in this world.

＊　＊　＊

As the volume progresses into its third section, Celan lets religious
and metaphysical issues move to the foreground. A poem like

---

3 Especially if Celan also knew Frost's remarkable poem, "To
Earthward."

"Tenebrae," cast in the form of a prayer, confronts a God who would let something like the Shoah happen. Again, Celan uses an earlier German poet, in this case Friedrich Hölderlin, to define his different situation in the middle of the twentieth century. Hölderlin's poem "Patmos" begins with the issue of proximity and the strangeness of any human/deity relationship:

> Close by, and difficult to grasp:
> That's the god.
> But where there's danger
> there's deliverance as well.[4]

For Celan, this problematic situation is reversed, seen from the other point of view:

> We're close at hand, Lord,
> so close you can grasp us.

But who, Celan seems to ask, would want to be grasped by a god? He is moving into a parodic treatment of the Incarnation:

> Grasped already, Lord,
> clawed into one another as if
> each of our bodies were also
> your body, Lord.

This feels like a dreadful mingling and confusion, and the Christian idea of sacrifice does not resolve the uneasiness it produces:

---

4 My translation (unpublished).

It was blood, it was
what you shed, Lord.

It gleamed.

It cast your likeness into our eyes . . .

In a poem that mimics psalms and prayers Celan lets the religious issues swirl around without ever arriving at belief or faith. God himself is instructed to "pray to us" and reminded that we are "close at hand." Unlike his friend Nelly Sachs, whose faith survived past the war, Celan can see no forgiveness for the deity and no comfort in addressing Him.

The natural world, on the other hand, offers occasional solace to the questioning sensibility of the poet. Celan and his family spent summer holidays in Brittany, and its coast, dunes, cliffs, and estuaries are cautiously celebrated as sustaining presences in poems like "White and Light" and "Matière de Bretagne." Throughout the book, nature affords greater peace than history or religion can muster, and quiet poems like "A Hand," "Sketch for a Landscape," and "Summer Report" bring Celan's love of nature to the foreground and offer readers relief from some of his more painful moments.

Always, though, in Celan there is a deliberate confusion of inner and outer worlds, so that it is never really possible to say that nature is distinct from interior discourse and from such states as nightmare and insomnia. The external world intrudes upon the dreaming, anguished consciousness, and vice versa. Sometimes the self finds relief, temporarily, and sometimes it is cast back into its own obsessions with the past and all its horrors and losses.

* * *

The volume closes, as it opened, with a sequence, "Stretto," that extends itself by means of a form in which each section's close provides the opening phrase for the next one, a kind of musical organization that relieves, even as it unfolds and expands upon, some of the speaker's inevitable sorrow and distress. It is moving and majestic, especially when read aloud.

The use of these longer sequences to open and close the volume speaks to Celan's careful organization of his collections and reiterates my contention, first articulated in my translation of his previous volume, *From Threshold to Threshold*, that the best way to understand this poet is through his collections, in their entirety and in terms of the order he made for the poems rather than in the selections that are so characteristic of previous translations. Working through the volumes, studying their progression and intertextual "conversing," has brought me much closer to a full understanding of Celan, and of course it is my hope that it will do the same for my readers.

In preparing this volume, the second in a projected group of three, I have been helped enormously by the responses and suggestions of many friends. Walter Strauss was the first person to critique my versions, and I regret that he did not live to see them in print. Subsequently, helped by a generous grant from the Mellon Foundation, I was able to organize productive work sessions with two colleagues, Stuart Friebert and Gert Niers. Their responses were invaluable, again and again, and their willingness to explore all aspects of Celan's language and his poetics made them indispensable readers. I have also had useful comments from Erin Moir, my student assistant under the grant, and from Thomas Wild, a former colleague. Ilya Kaminsky has been a most encouraging presence from the start, as have Jean Valentine, Deborah Bogen, and Franz Wright. And my publisher, Mariela Griffor, has been a model of patience and enthusiasm.

Oberlin, April 2012

I

Stimmen

I

Voices

Stimmen, ins Grün
der Wasserfläche geritzt.
Wenn der Eisvogel taucht,
sirrt die Sekunde:

Was zu dir stand
an jedem der Ufer,
es tritt
gemäht in ein anderes Bild.

*

Stimmen vom Nesselweg her:

Komm auf den Händen zu uns.
Wer mit der Lampe allein ist,
hat nur die Hand, draus zu lesen.

*

Stimmen, nachtdurchwachsen, Stränge,
an die du die Glocke hängst.

Wölbe dich, Welt:
Wenn die Totenmuschel heranschwimmt,
will es hier läuten.

Voices, etched
into the green of the water's surface.
When the kingfisher dives,
the moment vibrates:

What stood for you
on either bank,
it steps
mown down into another picture.

*

Voices from the nettle-path:

Come to us on your hands.
Whoever's alone with a lamp
has only a hand to read from.

*

Voices, night-veined, ropes
from which you hang the bell.

Arch yourself, world:
When the seashell of the dead washes up,
there will be bell-ringing.

*

Stimmen, vor denen dein Herz
ins Herz deiner Mutter zurückweicht.
Stimmen vom Galgenbaum her,
wo Spätholz und Frühholz die Ringe
tauschen und tauschen.

*

Stimmen, kehlig, im Grus,
darin auch Unendliches schaufelt,
(herz-)
schleimiges Rinnsal.

Setz hier die Boote aus, Kind,
die ich bemannte:

Wenn mittschiffs die Bö sich ins Recht setzt,
treten die Klammern zusammen.

*

*

Voices, that make your heart
turn back into your mother's heart.
Voices from the gallows-tree
where the wood-rings, old and new,
trade places.

*

Voices, raspy, in grit,
where even endlessness shovels
(heart-)
slime in rivulets.

Here, set the boats out, child,
the ones I manned:

When a squall takes over, amidships,
the hatches will batten.

*

Jakobsstimme:

Die Tränen.
Die Tränen im Bruderaug.
Eine blieb hängen, wuchs.
Wir wohnen darin.
Atme, daß
sie sich lose.

*

Stimmen im Innern der Arche:

Es sind
nur die Münder
geborgen. Ihr
Sinkenden, hört
auch uns.

*

Keine
Stimme – ein
Spätgeräusch, stundenfremd, deinen
Gedanken geschenkt, hier, endlich
herbeigewacht: ein
Fruchtblatt, augengroß, tief

Jacob's voice:

The tears.
The tears in my brother's eye.
One hung there, grew.
We live inside it.
Breathe, so it
can fall.

＊

Voices inside the Ark:

Only
the mouths
are sheltered. You
drowning ones, hear
us too.

＊

No
voice – a
late noise, alien to the hour, a
gift to your thoughts, brought here,
awakened at last: a
carpel, big as an eye,
deeply carved: it

geritzt; es
harzt, will nicht
vernarben.

oozes sap, it
won't scar over.

II

II

ZUVERSICHT

Es wird noch ein Aug sein,
ein fremdes, neben
dem unsern: stumm
unter steinernem Lid.

Kommt, bohrt euren Stollen!

Es wird eine Wimper sein,
einwärts gekehrt im Gestein,
von Ungeweintem verstählt,
die feinste der Spindeln.

Vor euch tut sie das Werk,
als gäb es, weil Stein ist, noch Brüder.

TRUST

There will be one more eye,
strange, next
to ours: silent
under a stony lid.

Come, drill your mineshaft!

There'll be an eyelash,
turned inward, in the rock,
steeled by what has not been wept,
the finest of spindles.

It does its work before you,
as if, because there's stone, there are still brothers.

MIT BRIEF UND UHR

Wachs,
Ungeschriebnes zu siegeln,
das deinen Namen
erriet,
das deinen Namen
verschlüsselt.

Kommst du nun, schwimmendes Licht?

Finger, wächsern auch sie,
durch fremde,
schmerzende Ringe gezogen.
Fortgeschmolzen die Kuppen.

Kommst du, schwimmendes Licht?

Zeitleer die Waben der Uhr,
bräutlich das Immentausend,
reisebereit.

Komm, schwimmendes Licht.

WITH LETTER AND CLOCK

Wax
to seal what never got written,
that guessed your
name,
that encodes
your name.

Will you come now, swimming light?

Fingers, wax too,
pulled through strange
painful rings.
Tips melted away.

Will you come now, swimming light?

The clock's honeycomb empty of time,
the thousand bees like brides,
ready to travel.

Come, swimming light.

UNTER EIN BILD

Rabenüberschwärmte Weizenwoge.
Welchen Himmels Blau? Des untern? Obern?
Später Pfeil, der von der Seele schnellte.
Stärkres Schwirren. Näh'res Glühen. Beide Welten.

UNDER A PICTURE

Ravenswarmed wheatsea.
Which heaven's blue? The one below? The one above?
Arrow that came later, shot from the soul.
Louder whirring. Nearer glowing. Both worlds.

HEIMKEHR

Schneefall, dichter und dichter,
taubenfarben, wie gestern,
Schneefall, als schliefst du auch jetzt noch.

Weithin gelagertes Weiß.
Drüberhin, endlos,
die Schlittenspur des Verlornen.

Darunter, geborgen,
stülpt sich empor,
was den Augen so weh tut,
Hügel um Hügel,
unsichtbar.

Auf jedem,
heimgeholt in sein Heute,
ein ins Stumme entglittenes Ich:
hölzern, ein Pflock.

Dort: ein Gefühl,
vom Eiswind herübergeweht,
das sein tauben-, sein schnee-
farbenes Fahnentuch festmacht.

HOMECOMING

Snowfall, thicker and thicker,
dove-colored, like yesterday,
snowfall, as if you were still asleep now.

Widely layered white.
On top of it, endlessly,
the sleigh-tracks of the lost.

Underneath, sheltered,
straining upward,
that which hurts the eyes,
hill after hill,
invisible.

On each,
brought home to its present,
an "I" that has slipped away into muteness:
wooden, a post.

There: a feeling,
blown over here on the icy wind,
fastening its dove-, its snow-
colored flag-cloth.

UNTEN

Heimgeführt ins Vergessen
das Gast-Gespräch unsrer
langsamen Augen.

Heimgeführt Silbe um Silbe, verteilt
auf die tagblinden Würfel, nach denen
die spielende Hand greift, groß,
im Erwachen.

Und das Zuviel meiner Rede:
angelagert dem kleinen
Kristall in der Tracht deines Schweigens.

BELOW

Brought home into forgetting,
the polite conversation
of our languid eyes.

Brought home syllable by syllable, distributed
among the day-blind dice, which
the throwing hand, huge, tries to grasp
while waking.

And the too-much of my speaking:
piled up around the little
crystal in the costume of your silence.

HEUTE UND MORGEN

So steh ich, steinern, zur
Ferne, in die ich dich führte:

Von Flugsand
ausgewaschsen die beiden
Höhlen am untern Stirnsaum.
Eräugtes
Dunkel darin.

Durchpocht
von schweigsam geschwungenen Hämmern
die Stelle,
wo mich das Flügelaug streifte.

Dahinter,
ausgespart in der Wand,
die Stufe,
drauf das Erinnerte hockt.

Hierher
sickert, von Nächten beschenkt,
eine Stimme,
aus der du den Trunk schöpfst.

TODAY AND TOMORROW

So I stand, turned to stone, facing
the distance into which I led you:

Drifting sand has washed out
both cavities below
the brow seam.
Darkness
glimpsed in there.

Knocked through
by silently swung hammers
the spot,
where the winged eye grazed me.

Behind,
notched in the wall,
the step
where what's remembered squats.

To this place
oozes, rewarded by nights,
a voice,
from which you can draw the drink.

SCHLIERE

Schliere im Aug:
von den Blicken auf halbem
Weg erschautes Verloren.
Wirklichgesponnenes Niemals,
wiedergekehrt.

Wege, halb – und die längsten.

Seelenbeschrittene Fäden,
Glasspur,
rückwärtsgerollt
und nun
vom Augen-Du auf dem steten
Stern über dir
weiß überschleiert.

Schliere im Aug:
daß bewahrt sei
ein durchs Dunkel getragenes Zeichen,
vom Sand (oder Eis?) einer fremden
Zeit für ein fremderes Immer
belebt und als stumm
vibrierender Mitlaut gestimmt.

STREAK

Streak in the eye:
something lost
half-way glimpsed when looking.
A true-spun Never has
come back again.

Ways, half-way – and the longest ones.

Threads stepped on the soul,
trace of glass
rolled backwards
and now
by your very eyes
veiled white
on a steady star above you.

Streak in the eye:
so that a sign
be preserved,
dragged through darkness,
restored to life by sand (or ice?)
of a strange time for an even stranger Always
and tuned to be a silently
vibrating consonant.

III

III

TENEBRAE

Nah sind wir, Herr,
nahe und greifbar.

Gegriffen schon, Herr,
ineinander verkrallt, als wär
der Leib eines jeden von uns
dein Leib, Herr.

Bete, Herr,
bete zu uns,
wir sind nah.

Windschief gingen wir hin,
gingen wir hin, uns zu bücken
nach Mulde und Maar.

Zur Tränke gingen wir, Herr.

Es war Blut, es war,
was du vergossen, Herr.

Es glänzte.

Es warf uns dein Bild in die Augen, Herr.
Augen und Mund stehn so offen und leer, Herr.
Wir haben getrunken, Herr.
Das Blut und das Bild, das im Blut war, Herr.

Bete, Herr.
Wir sind nah.

TENEBRAE

We're close at hand, Lord,
so close you can grasp us.

Grasped already, Lord,
clawed into one another as if
each of our bodies were also
your body, Lord.

Pray, Lord,
pray to us,
we're close by.

Slanted against the wind we went there,
went there so we might bend
over each pit and crater.

Went to the water-hole, Lord.

It was blood, it was
what you shed, Lord.

It shone.

It cast your likeness into our eyes, Lord.
Eyes open, mouth open, open and empty, Lord.
We have drunk, Lord.
The blood and the likeness that was in the blood, Lord.

Pray, Lord.
We're close by.

BLUME

Der Stein.
Der Stein in der Luft, dem ich folgte.
Dein Aug, so blind wie der Stein.

Wir waren
Hände,
wir schöpften die Finsternis leer, wir fanden
das Wort, das den Sommer heraufkam:
Blume.

Blume – ein Blindenwort.
Dein Aug und mein Aug:
sie sorgen
für Wasser.

Wachstum.
Herzwand um Herzwand
blättert hinzu.

Ein Wort noch, wie dies, und die Hämmer
schwingen im Freien.

FLOWER

The stone.
The stone in the air, which I followed.
Your eye, as blind as the stone.

We were
hands,
we scooped the darkness empty, we found
the word that came up in summer:
flower.

Flower – word for the blind.
Your eye and my eye:
they take care
of the water.

Growth.
Heartwall to heartwall,
make more petals.

One word more like this one, and the hammers
will swing in the air.

WEISS UND LEICHT

Sicheldünen, ungezählt.

Im Windschatten, tausendfach: du.
Du und der Arm,
mit dem ich nackt zu dir hinwuchs,
Verlorne.

Die Strahlen. Sie wehn uns zuhauf.
Wir tragen den Schein, den Schmerz und den Namen.

Weiß,
was sich uns regt,
ohne Gewicht,
was wir tauschen.
Weiß und Leicht:
laß es wandern.

Die Fernen, mondnah, wie wir. Sie bauen.
Sie bauen die Klippe, wo
sich das Wandernde bricht,
sie bauen
weiter:
mit Lichtschaum und stäubender Welle.

Das Wandernde, klippenher winkend.
Die Stirnen
winkt es heran,
die Stirnen, die man uns lieh,
um der Spiegelung willen.

WHITE AND LIGHT

Sickle-dunes, countless.

In wind-shadow, a thousand times: you.
You and the arm with which
I grew naked toward you,
lost one.

Rays of light. They blow us into a heap.
We bear the shine, the pain, the name.

White,
what stirs us,
weightless,
what we barter.
White and light:
let it roam.

The distances, moon-close, are like us. They build.
They build the cliff where
the wandering breaks,
they continue
to build:
with light-spume and wave-spray.

The wandering, signaling from cliffs.
It beckons
the foreheads
the foreheads that were lent to us
for the sake of mirroring.

Die Stirnen.
Wir rollen mit ihnen dorthin.
Stirnengestade.

Schläfst du?

Schlaf.

Meermühle geht,
eishell und ungehört,
in unsern Augen.

The foreheads.
We roll with them over there.
Coast of foreheads.

Are you asleep?

Sleep.

The mill of the ocean turns,
ice-bright, unheard
in our eyes.

SPRACHGITTER

Augenrund zwischen den Stäben.

Flimmertier Lid
rudert nach oben,
gibt einen Blick frei.

Iris, Schwimmerin, traumlos und trüb:
der Himmel, herzgrau, muß nah sein.

Schräg, in der eisernen Tülle,
der blakende Span.
Am Lichtsinn
errätst du die Seele.

(Wär ich wie du. Wärst du wie ich.
Standen wir nicht
unter *einem* Passat?
Wir sind Fremde.)

Die Fliesen. Darauf,
dicht beieinander, die beiden
herzgrauen Lachen:
zwei
Mundvoll Schweigen.

LANGUAGE BEHIND BARS

Round eye between bars.

Animal-like, the eyelid
flutters upward,
a glance breaks free.

Iris, that swimmer, dreamless, and drab:
the heavens, heart-gray, must be close by.

Slantwise, in the iron socket,
a smoldering shaving.
You find the soul
by its sense of light.

(If I were like you. Or you like me.
Didn't we stand
under one single tradewind?
We're strangers.)

Flagstones. On them,
close together, both
heart-gray puddles:
two
mouthfuls of silence.

SCHNEEBETT

Augen, weltblind, im Sterbegeklüft: Ich komm,
Hartwuchs im Herzen.
Ich komm.

Mondspiegel Steilwand. Hinab.
(Atemgeflecktes Geleucht. Strichweise Blut.
Wölkende Seele, noch einmal gestaltnah.
Zehnfingerschatten – verklammert.)

Augen weltblind,
Augen im Sterbegeklüft,
Augen Augen:

Das Schneebett unter uns beiden, das Schneebett.
Kristall um Kristall,
zeittief gegittert, wir fallen,
wir fallen und liegen und fallen.

Und fallen:
Wir waren. Wir sind.
Wir sind ein Fleisch mit der Nacht.
In den Gängen, den Gängen.

SNOW-BED

Eyes, world-blind, in the death-ravine: I'm coming,
hard growth forming in my heart.
I'm coming.

Moon-mirror cliff-face. Down.
(Shiny with breath-spots. Streaks of blood.
Clouding soul, coming back to the right shape.
Ten-fingered shadow – cramped.)

Eyes world-blind,
eyes in the death-ravine,
eyes eyes:

The snow-bed under us both, the snow-bed.
Crystal after crystal,
Barred deep in time, we're falling,
We fall and lie there and fall.

And fall:
We were. We are.
We and the night are one flesh,
In the passageways, the passageways.

WINDGERECHT

Tafelwand, grau, mit dem Nachtfries.
Felder, windgerecht, Raute bei Raute,
schriftleer.
Leuchtassel klettert vorbei.

Gesänge:
Augenstimmen, im Chor,
lesen sich wund.
(Ungewesen und Da,
beides zumal,
geht durch die Herzen.)

Später:
Schneewuchs durch alle Gehäuse, frei
ein einziges Feld,
das ein Lichtschein beziffert: die Stimmen.

Die Stimmen:
windgerecht, herznah,
brandbestattet.

ACCORDING TO THE WIND

Panel-wall, gray, with the night-frieze.
Fields, according to the wind, square after square,
empty of writing.
Light-tassel climbing past.

Chanting:
eye-voices, a choir,
read themselves sore.
(Never-existed and Here,
both at once,
going through the hearts.)

Later:
snow-growth through all vessels, just
one field free,
marked out by radiance: the voices.

The voices:
According to the wind, heart-close,
cremated.

NACHT

Kies und Geröll. Und ein Scherbenton, dünn,
als Zuspruch der Stunde.

Augentausch, endlich, zur Unzeit:
bildbeständig,
verholzt
die Netzhaut –:
das Ewigkeitszeichen.

Denkbar:
droben, im Weltgestänge,
sterngleich,
das Rot zweier Münder.

Hörbar (vor Morgen?): ein Stein,
der den andern zum Ziel nahm.

NIGHT

Gravel and pebbles. And a potsherd-sound, thin,
the hour's consolation.

Glance-trading, finally, mistimed:
picture-faithful,
retina
turned to wood — :
the sign of eternity.

Thinkable:
up there, among the universal system of levers,
starlike,
the redness of two mouths.

Audible (before dawn?): a stone,
that took the other as its target.

MATIÈRE DE BRETAGNE

Ginsterlicht, gelb, die Hänge
eitern gen Himmel, der Dorn
wirbt um die Wunde, es läutet
darin, es ist Abend, das Nichts
rollt seine Meere zur Andacht,
das Blutsegel hält auf dich zu.

Trocken, verlandet
das Bett hinter dir, verschilft
seine Stunde, oben,
beim Stern, die milchigen
Priele schwatzen im Schlamm, Steindattel,
unten, gebuscht, klafft ins Gebläu, eine Staude
Vergänglichkeit, schön,
grüßt dein Gedächtnis.

(Kanntet ihr mich,
Hände? Ich ging
den gegabelten Weg, den ihr wiest, mein Mund
spie seinen Schotter, ich ging, meine Zeit,
wandernde Wächte, warf ihren Schatten — kanntet ihr mich?)

Hände, die dorn-
umworbene Wunde, es läutet,
Hände, das Nichts, seine Meere,
Hände, im Ginsterlicht, das
Blutsegel
hält auf dich zu.

MATIÈRE DE BRETAGNE

Gorse-light, yellow, the slopes
fester toward heaven, the thorn
courts the wound, bells
tolling, it's evening, the Nothingness
rolls its seas toward worship,
the blood-sail's headed toward you.

Parched, silted up,
the riverbed behind you, its hour
choked with sedge, overhead,
next to the star, the milky
channels gabble in the mud, stone-mussels
down below, bushlike, gaping into blue, a shrub
of transience, lovely,
greets your memory.

(Did you know me,
hands? I walked
the forked path you showed me, my mouth
spitting its chippings, I walked, my time,
a wall of shifting snow
that cast its shadow – did you know me?)

Hands, the thorn-
courted wound, a bell tolling,
hands, the Nothingness, its seas,
hands, in the gorse-light, the
blood-sail
headed toward you.

Du
du lehrst
du lehrst deine Hände
du lehrst deine Hände du lehrst
du lehrst deine Hände
               schlafen

You
you teach
you teach your hands
you teach your hands you teach
you teach your hands
          to sleep

SCHUTTKAHN

Wasserstunde, der Schuttkahn
fährt uns zu Abend, wir haben,
wie er, keine Eile, ein totes
Warum steht am Heck.

....

Geleichtert. Die Lunge, die Qualle
bläht sich zur Glocke, ein brauner
Seelenfortsatz erreicht
das hellgeatmete Nein.

RUBBISH BARGE

Water-hour, the rubbish barge
carries us to evening, we have,
like it, no haste, a dead Why
stands at the stern.

....

Lightened. The lung, the jellyfish
swells into a bell, a brown
soul-extension reaches
the clear-breathed No.

IV

IV

KÖLN, AM HOF

Herzzeit, es stehn
die Geträumten für
die Mitternachtsziffer.

Einiges sprach in die Stille, einiges schwieg,
einiges ging seiner Wege.
Verbannt und Verloren
waren daheim.

Ihr Dome.

Ihr Dome ungesehn,
ihr Ströme unbelauscht,
ihr Uhren tief in uns.

COLOGNE, AT THE HOF

Heart-time, those dreamed about
stand for the midnight
cipher.

Something spoke in the silence, something
was still, something went its way.
What was banished and what was lost
were at home.

You cathedrals.

You cathedrals, unseen,
you rivers unheard,
you clocks deep inside us.

IN DIE FERNE

Stummheit, aufs neue, geräumig, ein Haus –:
komm, du sollst wohnen.

Stunden, fluchschön gestuft: erreichbar
die Freistatt.

Schärfer als je die verbliebene Luft: du sollst atmen,
atmen und du sein.

INTO THE DISTANCE

Muteness, spacious once more, a house —:
come on, you shall live there.

Hours, finely staggered, curse-lovely: with access to
the sanctuary.

Sharper than ever, the air that's left behind: you shall breathe,
breathe and be you.

EIN TAG UND NOCH EINER

Föhniges Du. Die Stille
flog uns voraus, ein zweites,
deutliches Leben.

Ich gewann, ich verlor, wir glaubten
an düstere Wunder, der Ast,
rasch an den Himmel geschrieben, trug uns, wuchs
durchs ziehende Weiß in die Mondbahn, ein Morgen
sprang ins Gestern hinauf, wir holten,
zerstoben, den Leuchter, ich stürzte
alles in niemandes Hand.

ONE DAY AND THEN ANOTHER

Chinook-like you. The stillness
flew on ahead of us, a second,
distinct life.

I won, I lost, we believed
in shadowy wonders, the branch,
quick-sketched on the sky, carried us, it grew
through drifting white into the moon's orbit,
a tomorrow leaped up into yesterday, we
got hold of the candlestick, pulverized, I dumped
everything into nobody's hand.

IN MUNDHÖHE

In Mundhöhe, fühlbar:
Finstergewächs.

(Brauchst es, Licht, nicht zu suchen, bleibst
das Schneegarn, hältst
deine Beute.

Beides gilt:
Berührt und Unberührt.
Beides spricht mit der Schuld von der Liebe,
beides will dasein und sterben.)

Blattnarben, Knospen, Gewimper.
Äugendes, tagfremd.
Schelfe, wahr und offen.

Lippe wußte. Lippe weiß.
Lippe schweigt es zu Ende.

AT MOUTH LEVEL

At mouth level, palpable:
dark growth.

(Light, you do not need to seek it, you
remain the snow-snare, holding
your prey.

Both are valid:
the touched and the untouched.
Both speak about love with guilt,
both want being and want to die.)

Leaf-scars, buds, eye-lashes.
Eye-glimpse, day-strange.
Husk, true and open.

Lip knew. Lip knows.
Lip is silent about it, to the end.

EINE HAND

Der Tisch, aus Stundenholz, mit
dem Reisgericht und dem Wein.
Es wird
geschwiegen, gegessen, getrunken.

Eine Hand, die ich küßte,
leuchtet den Mündern.

A HAND

A table, made of hour-wood, with
the rice dish and the wine.
There's
silence, eating, drinking.

A hand, that I kissed,
lights the way for the mouths.

ABER

(Du
fragst ja, ich
sags dir:)

Strahlengang, immer, die
Spiegel, nachtweit, stehn
gegeneinander, ich bin,
hingestoßen zu dir, eines
Sinnes mit diesem
Vorbei.

Aber: mein Herz
ging durch die Pause, es wünscht dir
das Aug, bildnah und zeitstark,
das mich verformt —:

die Schwäne,
in Genf, ich sah's nicht, flogen, es war,
als schwirrte, vom Nichts her, ein Wurfholz
ins Ziel einer Seele: soviel
Zeit
denk mir, als Auge, jetzt zu:
daß ichs
schwirren hör, näher – nicht
neben mir, nicht,
wo du nicht sein kannst.

BUT

(Since you
are asking, I'll
tell you:)

Shining path, always, the
mirrors, wide as night, stand
opposite each other, I am,
shoved toward you, of
one mind with this
over-and-done-with.

But: my heart
went through the hiatus, wishing you
the eye, picture-close and time-strong,
that distorts me – :

the swans
in Geneva, I didn't see, flew, it was
as if there whirred out of nothingness a throwing stick
whizzing into the target of the soul: so much
time
allow me now, as an eye:
so that I
may hear it whir, nearer – not
next to me, not
where you cannot be.

ALLERSEELEN

Was hab ich
getan?
Die Nacht besamt, als könnt es
noch andere geben, nächtiger als
diese.

Vogelflug, Steinflug, tasuend
beschriebene Bahnen. Blicke,
geraubt und gepflückt. Das Meer,
gekostet, vertrunken, verträumt. Eine Stunde,
seelenverfinstert. Die nächste, ein Herbstlicht,
dargebracht einem blinden
Gefühl, das des Wegs kam. Andere, viele,
ortlos und schwer aus sich selbst: erblickt und umgangen.
Findlinge, Sterne,
schwarz und voll Sprache: benannt
nach zerschwiegenem Schwur.

Und einmal (wann? auch dies ist vergessen):
den Widerhaken gefühlt,
wo der Puls den Gegentakt wagte.

ALL SOULS

What have I
done?
Seeded the night, as if
there could be others, even more night-like
than this one.

Bird flight, stone flight, a thousand
described paths. Glances,
stolen and plucked. The sea,
tasted, drunk empty, dreamed away. One hour,
soul-eclipsed. The next one, an autumn light
offered as alms to a blind
feeling, encountered on the road. Other hours, many,
placeless and heavy with themselves: glimpsed and skirted.
Erratics, stars,
black and full of speech: named
after an oath pressed into silence.

And once (when? this too is forgotten):
the barbed hook, felt
when the pulse dared its counter beat.

ENTWURF EINER LANDSCHAFT

Rundgräber, unten. Im
Viertakt der Jahresschritt auf
den Steilstufen rings.

Laven, Basalte, weltherz-
durchglühtes Gestein.
Quelltuff,
wo uns das Licht wuchs, vor
dem Atem.

Ölgrün, meerdurchstäubt die
unbetretbare Stunde. Gegen
die Mitte zu, grau,
ein Steinsattel, drauf,
gebeult und verkohlt,
die Tierstirn mit
der strahligen Blesse.

SKETCH FOR A LANDSCAPE

Circular graves, below. In
quarter time, the year's pace on
the steep surrounding steps.

Lavas, basalts, stone
from the world's heart, glowing.
Tufa welling up
where light grew for us, before
our breath.

Oil-green, the sea-sprayed
inaccessible hour. Gray
toward the center,
a stone saddle, on top,
dented and charred,
the animal brow with
the radiant blaze.

V

V

EIN AUGE, OFFEN

Stunden, maifarben, kühl.
Das nicht mehr zu Nennende, heiß,
hörbar im Mund.

Niemandes Stimme, wieder.

Schmerzende Augapfeltiefe:
das Lid
steht nicht im Wege, die Wimper
zählt nicht, was eintritt.

Die Träne, halb,
die schärfere Linse, beweglich,
holt dir die Bilder.

AN EYE, OPEN

Hours, May-colored, cool.
The no-longer-nameable, hot,
audible in the mouth.

Nobody's voice, once again.

Painful depth of eyeball:
the lid
is not in the way, the lash
does not keep track of what goes in.

The tear, half,
the sharper lens, mobile,
brings you the pictures.

OBEN, GERÄUSCHLOS, die
Fahrenden: Geier und Stern.

Unten, nach allem, wir,
zehn an der Zahl, das Sandvolk. Die Zeit,
wie denn auch nicht, sie hat
auch für uns eine Stunde, hier,
in der Sandstadt.

(Erzähl von den Brunnen, erzähl
von Brunnenkranz, Brunnenrad, von
Brunnenstuben – erzähl.

Zähl und erzähl, die Uhr,
auch diese, läuft ab.

Wasser: welch
ein Wort. Wir verstehen dich, Leben.)

Der Fremde, ungebeten, woher,
der Gast.
Sein triefendes Kleid.
Sein triefendes Auge.

(Erzähl uns von Brunnen, von –
Zähl und erzähl.
Wasser: welch
ein Wort.)

OVERHEAD, NOISELESS, those
travelers: vulture and star.

Below, after everything, we,
the sand-people, ten in number. Time,
and why shouldn't it?, has
an hour for us as well, here
in the sand-city.

(Tell about the wells, tell
about the well-wreath, the well-wheel, the
well-cisterns – tell it all.

Count and account, the clock,
even this one, runs down.

Water: what
a word. We understand you, life.)

The stranger, unbidden, from where,
the guest.
His dripping garment.
His dripping eye.

(Tell us about wells, about —
count and account.
Water: what
a word.)

Sein Kleid-und-Auge, er steht,
wie wir, voller Nacht, er bekundet
Einsicht, er zählt jetzt,
wie wir, bis zehn
und nicht weiter.

Oben, die
Fahrenden
bleiben
unhörbar.

His garment-and-eye, he stands,
like us, full of night, he vouchsafes
insight, he counts now,
as we do, up to ten
and no further.

Overhead, the
travelers
remain
inaudible.

DIE WELT, zu uns
in die leere Stunde getreten:

Zwei
Baumschäfte, schwarz,
unverzweigt, ohne
Knoten.
In der Düsenspur, scharfrandig, das
eine frei-
stehende Hochblatt.

Auch wir hier, im Leeren,
stehn bei den Fahnen.

THE WORLD, joining us
during the empty hour:

Two
tree trunks, black,
not branching, without
knots.
In the jet's contrail, sharp edged, the
one free-
standing flower-leaf.

We too, here in the emptiness,
stand by the banners.

EIN HOLZSTERN, blau,
aus kleinen Rauten gebaut. Heute, von
der jüngsten unserer Hände.

Das Wort, während
du Salz aus der Nacht fällst, der Blick
wieder die Windgalle sucht:

– Ein Stern, tu ihn,
tu den Stern in die Nacht.

(– In meine, in
meine.)

A WOODSTAR, blue,
built of small facets. Today,
by the youngest of our hands.

The word, while
you cut salt out of the night, the glance
seeking the windgall again:

—A star, put it,
put the star into the night.

(—Into mine, into
mine.)

SOMMERBERICHT

Der nicht mehr beschrittene, der
umgangene Thymianteppich.
Eine Leerzeile, quer
durch die Glockenheide gelegt.
Nichts in den Windbruch getragen.

Wieder Begegnungen mit
vereinzelten Worten wie:
Steinschlag, Hartgräser, Zeit.

SUMMER REPORT

The no longer walked-on, the
avoided carpet of thyme.
A blank line
slanted through the bell-heather.
Carried nothing into the windfall.

Once more, encounters with
scattered words like:
rockfall, strawgrass, time.

NIEDRIGWASSER. Wir sahen
die Seepocke, sahen
die Napfschnecke, sahen
die Nägel an unsern Händen.
Niemand schnitt uns das Wort von der Herzwand.

(Fährten der Strandkrabbe, morgen,
Kriechfurchen, Wohngänge, Wind-
zeichnung im grauen
Schlick. Feinsand,
Grobsand, das
von den Wänden Gelöste, bei
andern Hartteilen, im
Schill.)

Ein Aug, heute,
gab es dem zweiten, beide,
geschlossen, folgten der Strömung zu
ihrem Schatten, setzten
die Fracht ab (*niemand
schnitt uns das Wort von der* – –), bauten
den Haken hinaus – eine Nehrung, vor
ein kleines
unbefahrbares Schweigen.

LOW-LYING WATER. We saw
the sea-pock, saw
the basin-snail, saw
the nails on our hands.
Nobody cut the word from our heart walls.

(Tracks of the sand crab, tomorrow,
creep-furrows, hideouts, wind
sketches in the gray
muck. Fine sand,
coarse sand, that
came loose from the walls, next to the other
hard parts, in the
shell fragments.)

One eye, today,
gave it to the other one, both,
closed, followed the current to
their shadow, deposited
the freight *(nobody
cut our word from the —)*, built
the hook outward – a spit of land, before
a small
impassable silence.

BAHNDÄMME, WEGRÄNDER, ÖDPLÄTZE, SCHUTT

Lichtgewinn, meßbar, aus
Distelähnlichem:
einiges
Rot, im Gespräch
mit einigem Gelb.
Die Luftschleier vor
deinem verzweifelten Aug.
Das letzte
reitende Sandkorn.

(Die
Augärten, damals, das
gelächelte Wort
vom Marchfeld, vom
Steppengras dort.
Das tote Ringelspiel, kling.
Wir
drehten uns weiter.)

Der Sandkornritt, das
Auge, ihm zugewandt.
Die Stundentür und
ihre Geräusche.

RAILWAY EMBANKMENTS, ROADSIDES, VACANT LOTS,
RUBBISH

Gain of light, measurable, from
something like a thistle:
some
red, conversing
with some yellow.
The air-haze before
your despairing eye.
The last
riding sand grain.

(The
Vienna gardens*, back then, the
smiled word
about Marchfeld, the
steppe grass there.
The dead carousel, clink.
We
kept on turning.)

The sand grain ride, the
eye, turned toward it.
The hour-door and
its sounds.

(*The German is *Augärten*, a large park in Vienna. Marchfeld is a
plain in Austria, scene of many battles.)

ENGFÜHRUNG

STRETTO

*

VERBRACHT ins
Gelände
mit der untrüglichen Spur:

Gras, auseinandergeschrieben. Die Steine, weiß,
mit den Schatten der Halme:
Lies nicht mehr – schau!
Schau nicht mehr – geh!

Geh, deine Stunde
hat keine Schwestern, du bist –
bist zuhause. Ein Rad, langsam,
rollt aus sich selber, die Speichen
klettern,
klettern auf schwärzlichem Feld, die Nacht
braucht keine Sterne, nirgends
fragt es nach dir.

*

Nirgends
fragt es nach dir –

Der Ort, wo sie lagen, er hat
einen Namen – er hat
keinen. Sie lagen nicht dort. Etwas
lag zwischen ihnen. Sie
sahn nicht hindurch.

Brought forcibly to
the terrain with
the unmistakable trace:

Grass, written asunder. The stones, white,
with the shadows of grassblades:
Read no more – watch!
Watch no more – go!

Go, your hour
has no sisters, you are –
are at home. A wheel, slowly,
rolls by itself, the spokes
climb,
climb on a field of blackness, the night
needs no stars, nowhere
is anything asking for you.

*

Nowhere
is anything asking for you –

The place, where they lay, it has
a name – it has
none. They didn't lie there. Something
lay between them. They
couldn't see through it

Sahn nicht, nein,
redeten von
Worten. Keines
erwachte, der
Schlaf
kam über sie.

                                Kam, kam. Nirgends
                                        fragt es –

Ich bins, ich,
ich lag zwischen euch, ich war
offen, war
hörbar, ich tickte euch zu, euer Atem
gehorchte, ich
bin es noch immer, ihr
schlaft ja.

*

Didn't see, no,
spoke of
words. None
woke,
sleep
came over them.
                    Came, came. Nowhere
                        is anything asking –
I'm the one, I,
I lay between you, I was
open, was
audible, I ticked at you, your breath
obeyed, I'm
still the same, you
are really asleep.

*

                                        Bin es noch immer –

Jahre.
Jahre, Jahre, ein Finger
tastet hinab und hinan, tastet
umher:
Nahtstellen, fühlbar, hier
klafft es weit auseinander, hier
wuchs es wieder zusammen – wer
deckte es zu?

        *

                                        Deckte es
                                                zu – wer?

Kam, kam.
Kam ein Wort, kam,
kam durch die Nacht,
wollt leuchten, wollt leuchten.

Asche.
Asche, Asche.
Nacht.
Nacht-und-Nacht. – Zum
Aug geh, zum feuchten.

        *

                                        I'm still the same –

Years.
Years, years, a finger
fumbles up and down, fumbles
around:
seams, palpable, here
it's split wide open, here
it grew together again – who
covered it up?

*

                                    Covered it
                                        up – who?

Came, came.
A word came, came,
came through the night,
wanted to glow, wanted to glow.

Ashes.
Ashes, ashes.
Night.
Night-and-night. – Go
to the eye, the wet one.

*

Zum

Aug geh,

zum feuchten –

Orkane.
Orkane, von je,
Partikelgestöber, das andre,
du
weißts ja, wir
lasens im Buche, war
Meinung.

War, war
Meinung. Wie
faßten wir uns
an – an mit
diesen
Händen?

Es stand auch geschrieben, daß.
Wo? Wir
taten ein Schweigen darüber,
giftgestillt, groß,
ein
grünes
Schweigen, ein Kelchblatt, es
hing ein Gedanke an Pflanzliches dran –
grün, ja
hing, ja,
unter hämischem
Himmel.

                        Go
                                    to the eye,
                                                the wet one –

Hurricanes.
Hurricanes, from the past,
particle storm, the other,
you
know it, we
read in the book, it was
opinion.

Was, was
opinion. How
did we touch
each other – each other with
these
hands?

And it was written, that.
Where? We
pulled a silence over it,
poison-quieted, great,
a
green
silence, a sepal, a
thought of plants hung there –
green, yes,
hung, yes,
under a spiteful
sky.

An, ja,
Pflanzliches.

Ja.
Orkane, Par-
tikelgestöber, es blieb
Zeit, blieb,
es beim Stein zu versuchen – er
war gastlich, er
fiel nicht ins Wort. Wie
gut wir es hatten:

Körnig,
körnig und faserig. Stengelig,
dicht;
traubig und strahlig; nierig,
plattig und
klumpig; locker, ver-
ästelt —: er, es
fiel nicht ins Wort, es
sprach,
sprach gerne zu trockenen Augen, eh es sie schloß.

Sprach, sprach.
War, war.

Wir
ließen nicht locker, standen
inmitten, ein
Porenbau, und
es kam.

Of, yes,
plants.

Yes.
Hurricanes, part-
icle storms, there was
time, still,
to try it out with the stone — it was
hospitable, it
didn't interrupt. How
good we had it:

Grainy,
grainy and stringy. Stalked,
thick;
clustered and radiant; kidney-shaped,
level and
bumpy; loose, branch-
ing --: it
did not interrupt, it
spoke,
spoke gladly to dry eyes, before it shut them.

Spoke, spoke.
Was, was.

We
didn't let go, we stood
in the midst of it, a
porous shelter, and
it came.

Kam auf uns zu, kam
hindurch, flickte
unsichtbar, flickte
an der letzten Membran,
und
die Welt, ein Tausendkristall,
schoß an, schoß an.

*

                               Schoß an, schoß an.
                                       Dann –

Nächte, entmischt. Kreise,
grün oder blau, rote
Quadrate: die
Welt setzt ihr Innerstes ein
im Spiel mit den neuen
Stunden. – Kreise
rot oder schwarz, helle
Quadrate, kein
Flugschatten,
kein
Meßtisch, keine
Rauchseele steigt und spielt mit.

*

                               Steigt und
                                   spielt mit –

Came at us, came
through, mended
invisibly, mended
the last membrane, and
the world, a thousand-faced crystal,
shot out, shot out.

*

                                        Shot out, shot out.
                                                Then –

nights, dis-integrated. Circles,
green or blue, red
squares: the
world stakes its innermost being
on the game with the new
hours. – Circles,
red or black, bright
squares, no
flight shadow,
no
surveyor's table, no
smoke-soul rises and joins in.

*

                                        Rises and
                                            joins in ---

In der Eulenflucht, beim
versteinerten Aussatz,
bei
unsern geflohenen Händen, in
der jüngsten Verwerfung,
überm
Kugelfang an
der verschütteten Mauer:

sichtbar, aufs
neue: die
Rillen, die

Chöre, damals, die
Psalmen. Ho, ho-
sianna.

Also
stehen noch Tempel. Ein
stern
hat wohl noch Licht.
Nichts,
nichts ist verloren.

Ho-
sianna.

In der Eulenflucht, hier,
die Gespräche, taggrau,
der Grundwasserspuren.

In the owl-flight, by the
leprosy turned to stone,
by
our hands, fled, in
the youngest rejection,
above the
bullet-trap
at the wall buried under rubble:

visible, once
more: the
grooves, the

choirs, then, the
psalms. Ho, ho-
sanna.

Thus
temples still stand. A
star
surely has light.
Nothing,
Nothing is lost.

Ho-
sanna.

In the owl-flight, here,
the conversations, day-gray,
the ground water traces.

*

        (-- taggrau,
            der
                Grundwasserspuren –

Verbracht
ins Gelände
mit
der untrüglichen
Spur:

Gras.
Gras,
auseinandergeschrieben.)

*

                (—day-gray,
                  the
                      ground water traces —

brought forcibly
to the terrian
with
the unmistakable
trace:

Grass.
Grass,
written asunder.)

CPSIA information can be obtained at www.ICGtesting.com
Printed in the USA
BVOW08s2216090214

344336BV00001B/49/P